# MATHS
# PHOTOCOPY
# MASTERS

## Peter Patilla

**Oxford University Press**

Oxford University Press, Great Clarendon Street, Oxford, OX2 6DP

*Oxford   New York   Athens*
*Auckland   Bangkok   Bogota   Bombay   Buenos Aires*
*Calcutta   Cape Town   Dar es Salaam   Delhi   Florence*
*Hong Kong   Istanbul   Karachi   Kuala Lumpur   Madras*
*Madrid   Melbourne   Mexico City   Nairobi   Paris*
*Singapore   Taipei   Tokyo   Toronto   Warsaw*

and associated companies in
*Berlin   Ibadan*

*Oxford* is a trade mark of Oxford University Press

First published 1997

ISBN 0 19 918612 X

Edited and prepared for publication by Paren & Stacey Editorial Consultants

Designed and produced by Gecko Limited, Bicester, Oxon

Printed in Great Britain by St Edmundsbury Press, Bury St Edmunds

Bound by Hunter and Foulis, Edinburgh

# CONTENTS

# Notes to accompany Maths Photocopy Masters: Book C

• These activities have been designed for children who are in their first year at school.

• The activities have been written using contexts from Stages 3, 4, and 5 of the *Oxford Reading Tree* although it is not necessary to have read any of the stories from these Stages in order to complete the activities.

• It is unrealistic to expect that maths and reading can progress in a matched way but the links to the stories are well worth using. Selected activities can be used as appropriate with the stories, either alongside the reading activity or in the context of maths teaching.

• The activities will supplement and complement any maths scheme a school uses, whether commercial or school developed.

• There is a progession through the activities in each of the mathematical areas of number, shape and data handling, although teachers may wish to reorganize some of the activities to match their own schemes of work. It is not intended that each child should undertake each sheet since the sheets are written as enrichment and practice activities to be used as appropriate. There is also a progression from Book A through Books B and C.

• Simple instructions are written on each sheet for an adult to read with the children. The tasks are intended to be done unaided by the children using simple recording techniques such as matching, ticking, circling, colouring and drawing.

• This book helps children to work towards or at the following levels:
Level 1 of the National Curriculum for England and Wales
Level A of the Scottish Curriculum Guidelines for 5-14
Level 1 of the Common Curriculum for Northern Ireland.

• The activities are suitable for use as part of a home-school links programme. The sheets can be taken home either for completion or after completion.

# Grid to show how each activity in Maths Photocopy Masters: Book C is related to the different aspects of the maths curriculum

| | number and number operations | patterns | shapes and position | measures | data handling | | number and number operations | patterns | shapes and position | measures | data handling | | number and number operations | patterns | shapes and position | measures | data handling |
|---|---|---|---|---|---|---|---|---|---|---|---|---|---|---|---|---|---|
| 1 | X | | | | | 21 | X | | | | | 41 | | | X | | |
| 2 | X | | | | | 22 | X | | | | | 42 | X | | X | | |
| 3 | X | | | | | 23 | X | | | | | 43 | X | | X | | |
| 4 | X | | | | | 24 | X | | | | | 44 | | | | X | |
| 5 | X | | | | | 25 | X | | | | | 45 | | | | X | |
| 6 | X | | | | | 26 | | X | X | | | 46 | | | | X | |
| 7 | X | | | | | 27 | | X | X | | | 47 | | | | X | |
| 8 | X | | | | | 28 | | X | X | | | 48 | | | | X | |
| 9 | X | | | | | 29 | | X | X | | | 49 | | | | X | |
| 10 | X | | | | | 30 | X | X | | | | 50 | | | | | X |
| 11 | X | | | | | 31 | X | X | | | | 51 | | | | | X |
| 12 | X | | | | | 32 | X | X | | | | 52 | | | | | X |
| 13 | X | | | | | 33 | X | X | | | | 53 | | | | | X |
| 14 | X | | | | | 34 | X | X | | | | 54 | | | | | X |
| 15 | X | | | | | 35 | X | X | | | | 55 | | | | | X |
| 16 | X | | | | | 36 | X | X | | | | 56 | | | | | X |
| 17 | X | | | | | 37 | X | X | | | | 57 | X | | | | |
| 18 | X | | | | | 38 | | | X | | | 58 | | X | X | | |
| 19 | X | | | | | 39 | | | X | | | 59 | | | X | | |
| 20 | X | | | | | 40 | | | X | | | | | | | | |

# Name _____

## Write the totals.

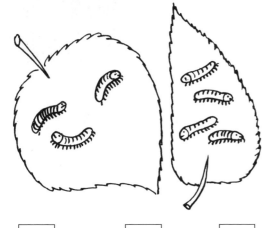

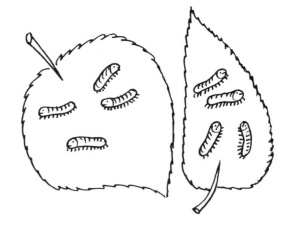

 and  → ☐

☐ and ☐ → ☐

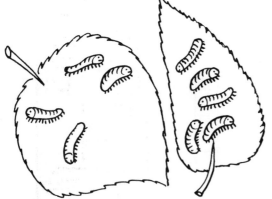

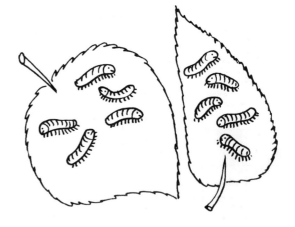

☐ and ☐ → ☐

☐ and ☐ → ☐

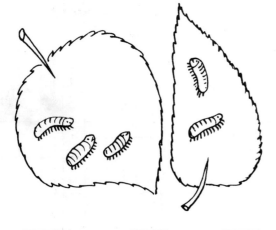

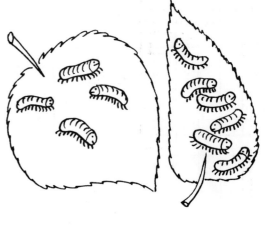

☐ and ☐ → ☐

☐ and ☐ → ☐

## Name

## Chip is adding stamps.
## Find the answers.

+ 2 →

+ 3 →

+ 6 →

+ 1 →

+ 4 →

+ 2 →

addition

**Name** _____

# Count the blocks.
# Write the sums.

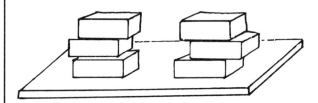

3 + 3 = ☐

☐ + ☐ = ☐

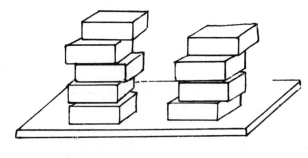

☐ + ☐ = ☐

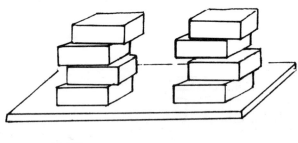

☐ + ☐ = ☐

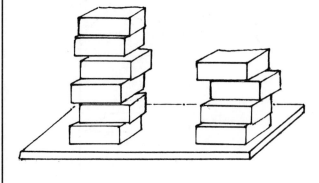

☐ + ☐ = ☐

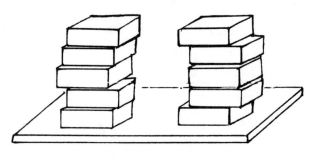

☐ + ☐ = ☐

# Name

## Match eggs to spoons.

8

6

5+0

6+2

4+2

10

5

8+1

3+1

9

7+3

4

## Write sums to match these spoons.

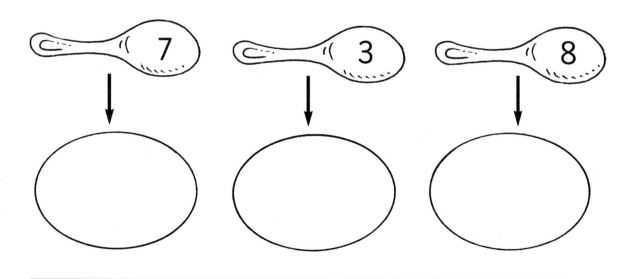

7

3

8

addition sums

# Name _____

## Match numbers to sums.

8   6

9

| 4+4 | 5+4 | 3+0 |
|-----|-----|-----|
| 4+2 | 9+1 | 5+2 |

10

7   3

5

9

6

10

8

| 5+3 | 2+3 | 2+2 |
|-----|-----|-----|
| 6+3 | 3+3 | 6+4 |

4

addition sums

## Name _____

# Write in the missing numbers.

4 count on 2 is ☐ .    1 count on 3 is ☐ .

2 count on 5 is ☐ .    5 count on 4 is ☐ .

3 count on 4 is ☐ .    6 count on 4 is ☐ .

# Write your own sums.

☐ count on ☐ is ☐ .

☐ count on ☐ is ☐ .

☐ count on ☐ is ☐ .

## Name

The frog jumps on the number track.

| 1 | 2 | 3 | 4 | 5 | 6 | 7 | 8 | 9 | 10 |

## Write where the frog lands.

## Write the sums.

| Start | Jump | Land | Sum |
|-------|------|------|-----|
| 3 | 3 | 6 | 3 + 3 = 6 |
| 1 | 5 | | |
| 7 | 3 | | |
| 4 | 4 | | |
| 2 | 8 | | |
| 5 | 4 | | |
| 6 | 3 | | |

Name

Biff uses vanishing cream.
She makes 2 things in each
row disappear.
Write how many are left.

Name _____

The birds take 3 plants from each row.
Write how many are left.

[ ]

[ ]

[ ]

[ ]

[ ]

Book C

taking away

# Write how many balls have gone into the pockets.

start            finish

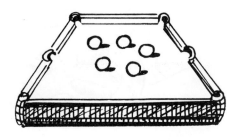 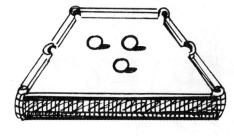

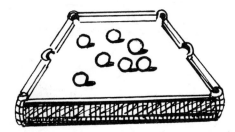 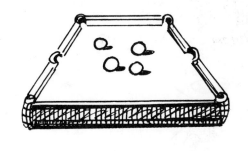

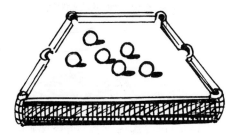 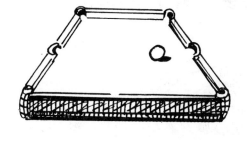

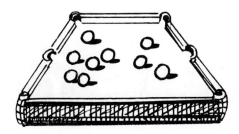 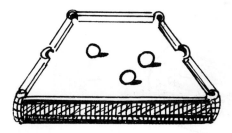

Book C        subtraction

# Name

The arrows show how many sausages have been eaten. Match to how many are left.

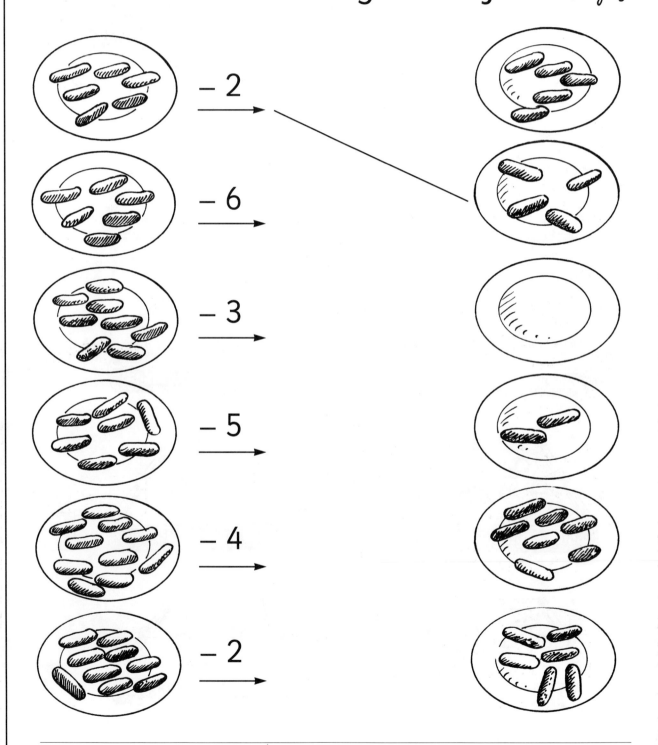

# Name

## How many birds have been scared away?
## Write a sum.

before                    after

                    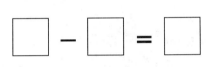

subtraction

Name _____

# Match arrows to targets.

8–3

9–7

3

2

6

10–6

5

7

4

7–4

7–0

9–3

# Write sums to match these targets.

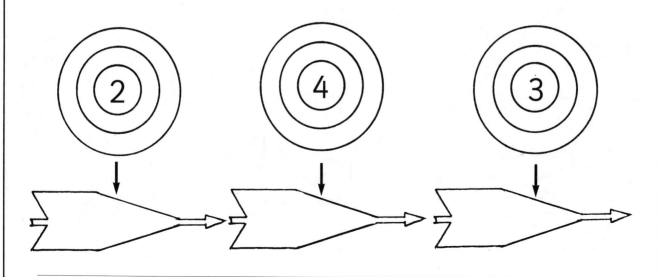

2

4

3

# Name

## Colour strawberries which match the jars.

subtraction sums

# Name

# Write in the missing numbers.

9

5

2

1

0

7 step back 2 is ☐ .

4 step back 3 is ☐ .

6 step back 3 is ☐ .

10 step back 4 is ☐ .

# Write your own sums.

☐ step back ☐ is ☐ .

☐ step back ☐ is ☐ .

☐ step back ☐ is ☐ .

☐ step back ☐ is ☐ .

# Name

## Write some sums.

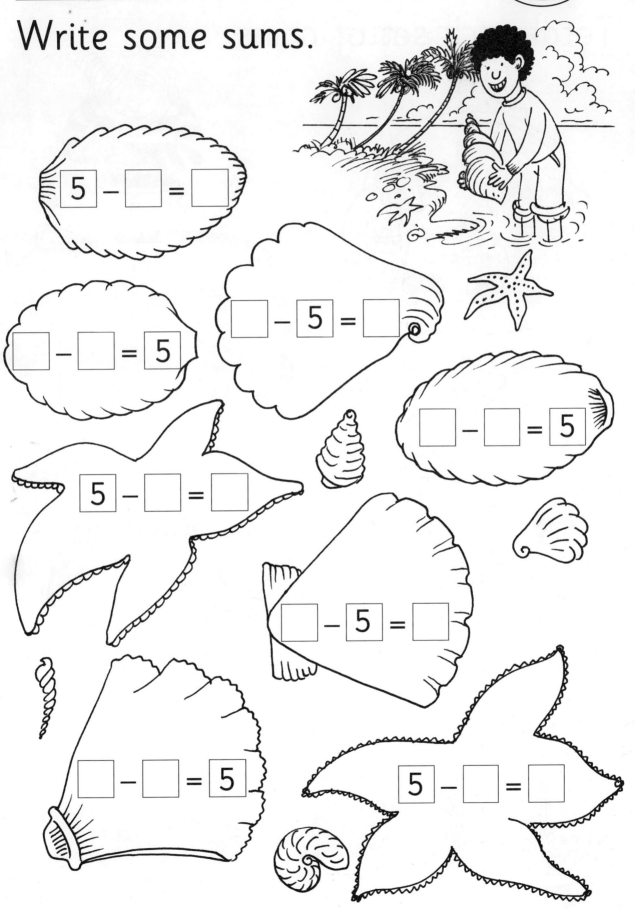

5 − □ = □

□ − □ = 5

□ − 5 = □

□ − □ = 5

5 − □ = □

□ − 5 = □

□ − □ = 5

5 − □ = □

subtraction sums

# Name

## Total each set of coins.

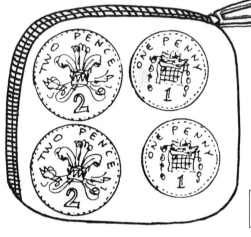

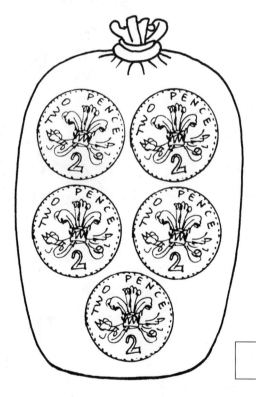

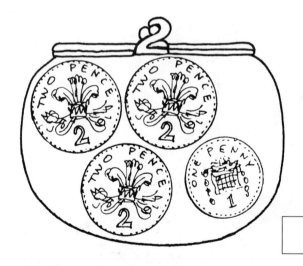

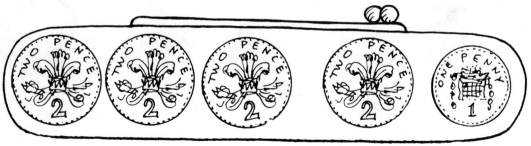

# Name

## Make fair swaps.
## Draw the coins.

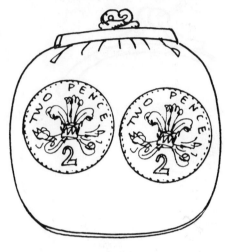 is the same as

 is the same as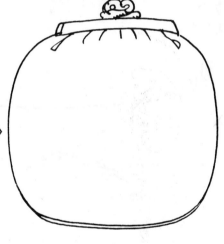

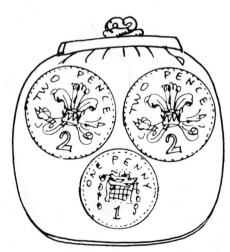 is the same as

coin equivalencies

Name _____

Draw some coins in each purse.

Write how much.

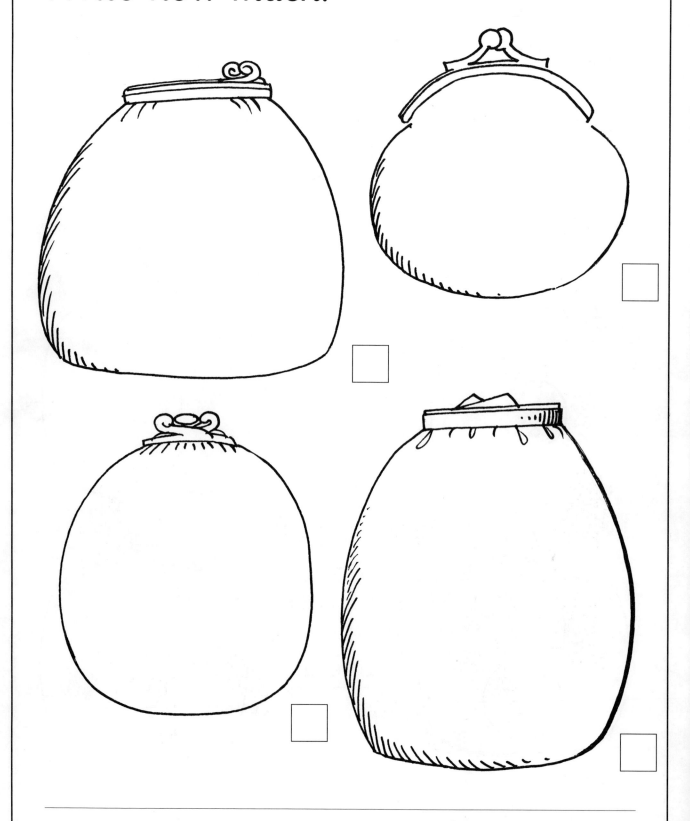

money: open task

# Name

## Kipper has 10p to spend.

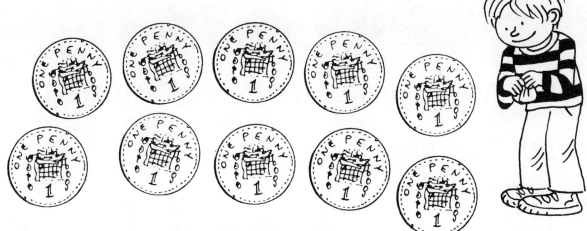

## What shall he buy?
## Write how much would be left.

## Name

Here are some trees in a line.

Write how many trees are hidden under the snow.

# Name

## Write how many elves.

4 more elves

How many? ☐

5 more elves

How many? ☐

3 fewer elves

How many? ☐

4 fewer elves

How many? ☐

2 more elves

How many? ☐

2 fewer elves

How many? ☐

How many children? ☐

How many beds? ☐

Each child wants a bed.

How many more beds are needed?

Draw them here.

number problem

Name _____

Do the sums.

Join the balloons with the same answer.

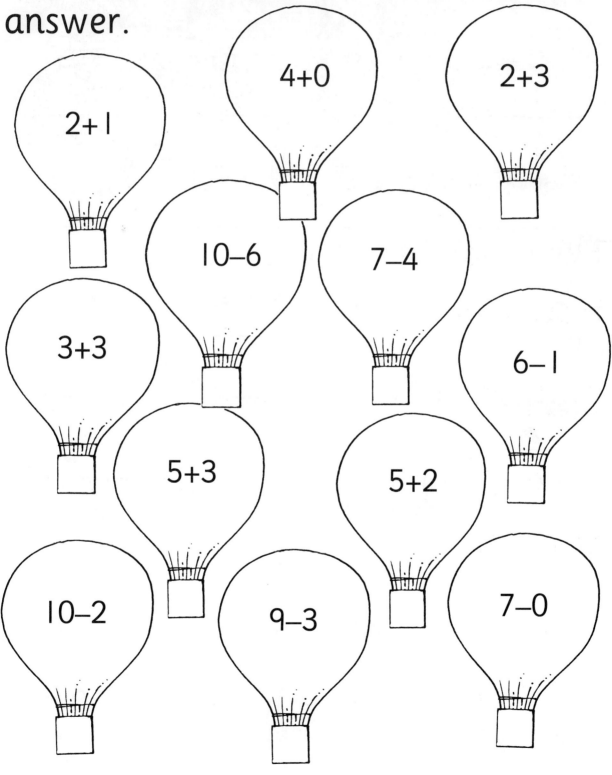

# Name

# Write numbers on the wagons.

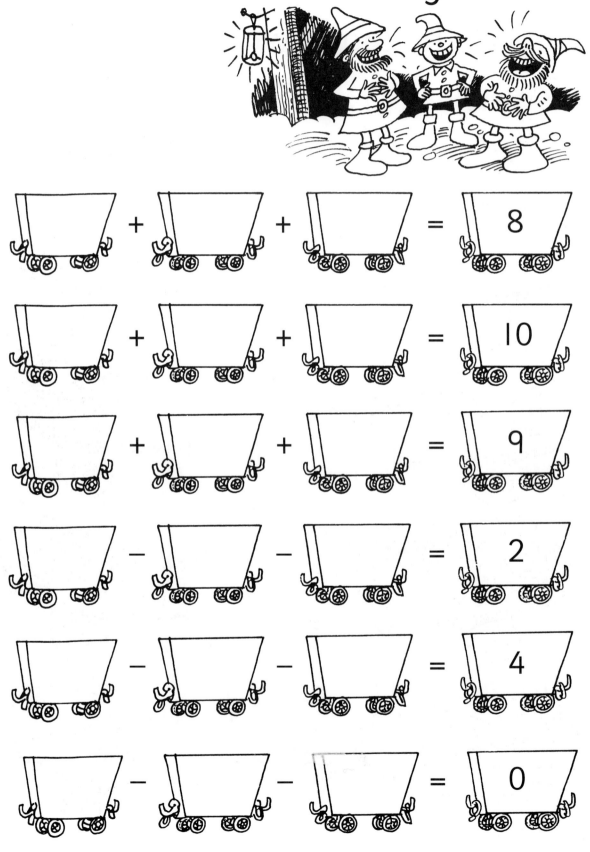

Book C

addition and subtraction sums

# Name

## Match the missing pieces.

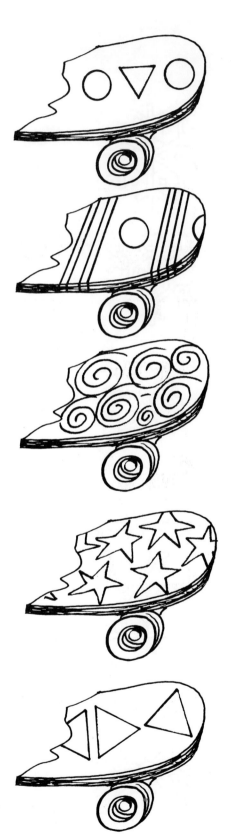

# Name

## Match the snowflakes.

# Name

## Draw in the missing pieces.

Name _____

# Continue each pattern.

Name _____

Activity
30

Dad

Mum

Biff

Chip

Kipper

Floppy

Who is first? ....................................................

Who is fifth? ....................................................

Who is second? ....................................................

Who is third? ....................................................

Who is fourth? ....................................................

Who is last? ....................................................

Book C

ordinal numbers

© OUP: this may be reproduced for class use solely within the purchaser's school or college

Count the toys. ☐

Count the tins. ☐    Count the books.

Which group has most? .............................................

.................................................................................

# Name

## Count the triangles on each dragon.

▢

▢

## Draw and count your own triangles.

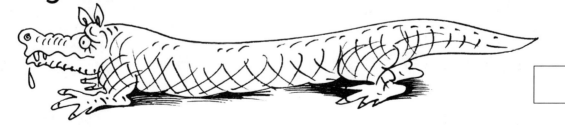

▢

## Colour the dragon with fewest triangles yellow.

**Name** _____

Start at 1 and join the dots in order.

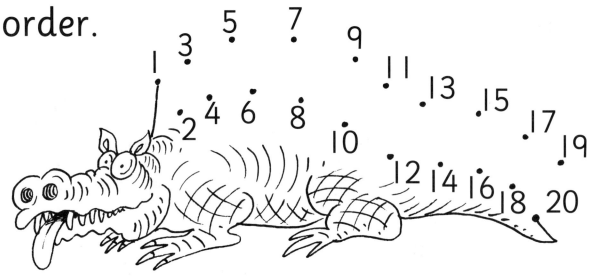

5    7
3        9
1          11
.13
2  4  6  8      .15
10        .17
.19
12 14 16 18  20

1

20  19

18.  .2      .3

.4

.5

17      16 8    7    6

14.      .9      .10
15

13      12      11

# Name

## Start at one and join the dots in order.

thirteen

eighteen
sixteen

twenty
one
nineteen
seventeen
fifteen   fourteen   twelve

three
ten

two   nine

four   six   eight   eleven

five   seven

Name _____

Find pairs of animals.
Join them.

There are ☐ pairs of animals.
There are ☐ animals altogether.

## Can you write in twos?

| 2 | | | | | | | | | 20 |
|---|---|---|---|---|---|---|---|---|---|

counting: number language

# Name

## Colour even numbers of bricks red.

  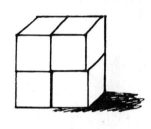

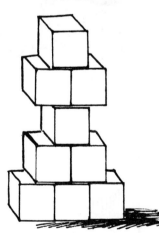 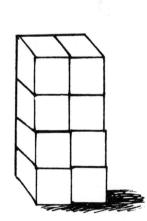 

## Write some even numbers.

Name

# Colour odd numbers of balls blue.

 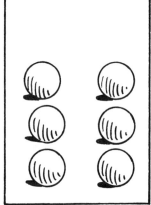 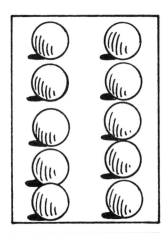

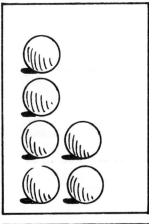 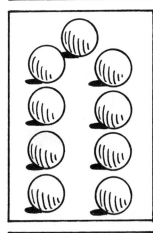 

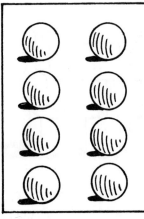 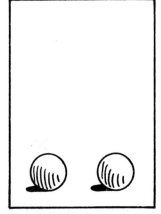 

# Write some odd numbers.

odd numbers

# Name _____

## Match names to shapes.

"Kipper's shape puzzle"

| | |
|---|---|
| circle | triangle | oval |
| square | diamond | rectangle |

names of 2D shapes

# Name _____

## Match stickers to names.

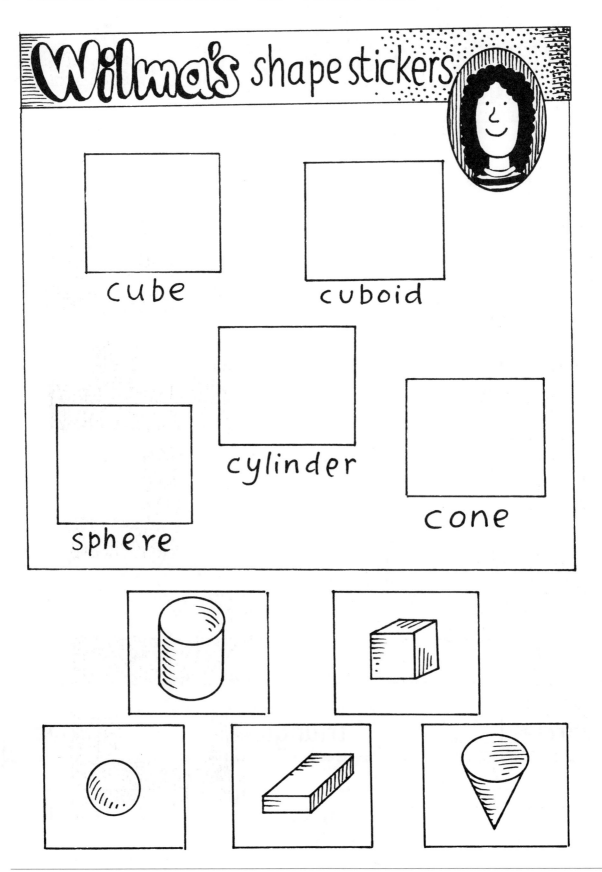

Wilma's shape stickers

cube

cuboid

cylinder

cone

sphere

names of 3D shapes

# Match shapes to shadows.

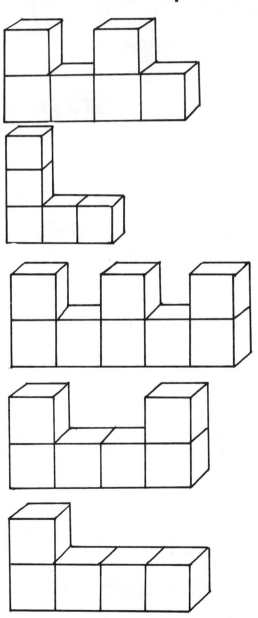

shape puzzle

# Name

## Find the salamander.

| |
|---|
| in front of the log |

| |
|---|
| between the flowers |

| |
|---|
| on top of the log |

| |
|---|
| behind the flowers |

| |
|---|
| inside the log |

| |
|---|
| under the log |

| |
|---|
| on a flower |

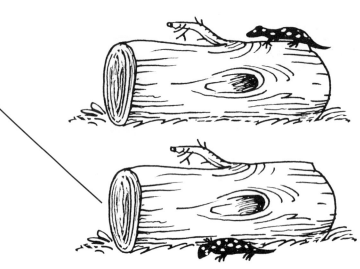

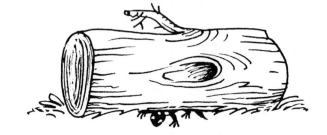

**Name** _____

Biff and Chip are sharing
each bun.

Colour Biff's half on each bun.

halving shapes

# Name

Chip used vanishing cream.

Half of each shape is missing.

Draw the missing half.

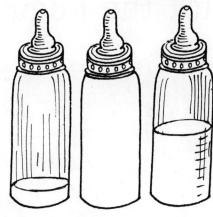

Tick the full bottle.

Tick the empty jar.

Tick the half-full bottle.

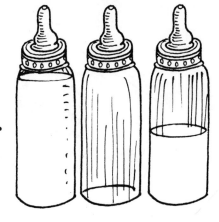

Colour one jar full.
Colour one jar half-full.

language of capacity

Name

## Tick the heavier babies.

## Tick the lighter babies.

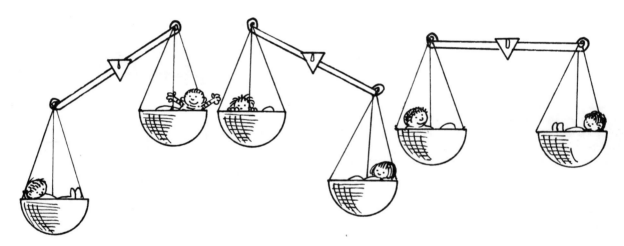

## Tick babies the same weight.

language of weight

Name _____

# Measure each belt in cm.

☐ cm

☐ cm

☐ cm

☐ cm

☐ cm

☐ cm

# Name _____

## Write the times.

☐ o'clock

☐ o'clock

☐ o'clock

☐ o'clock

Name _____

Write the missing numbers

on each clock.

Write the times.

_____ o'clock        _____ o'clock

Write the numbers.

Show a time on each clock.

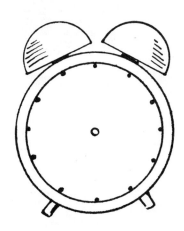 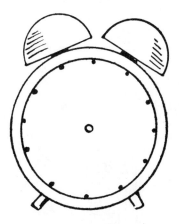

_____ o'clock        _____ o'clock

Name

Cut out the labels.

Put the days in order.

Stick them down.

Monday

Friday

Saturday

Wednesday

Thursday

Sunday

Tuesday

# Name

# Find and tally.          Total

| | | |
|---|---|---|
|  | I I I I | 4 |
| ⊙ | | |
| ◎ | | |
| 🧁 | | |

data: tallies

# Name

## Map labels to animals.

| has a beak | has 4 legs | has a long neck |
|:---:|:---:|:---:|

data: mapping diagram

**Name** _____

**Activity 52**

# Join the creepy-crawlies to the chart.

has 6 legs                    does not have 6 legs

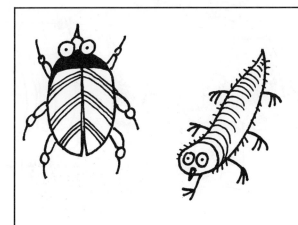

# Draw your own creepy-crawly in each part of the chart.

_____

Book C

data: Carroll diagram

# Name _____

## Join each person to the chart.

wearing nothing
on their head

wearing something
on their head

data: Venn diagram

# Name

## Look at each pirate.

## Tick or cross what is special about

## each one.

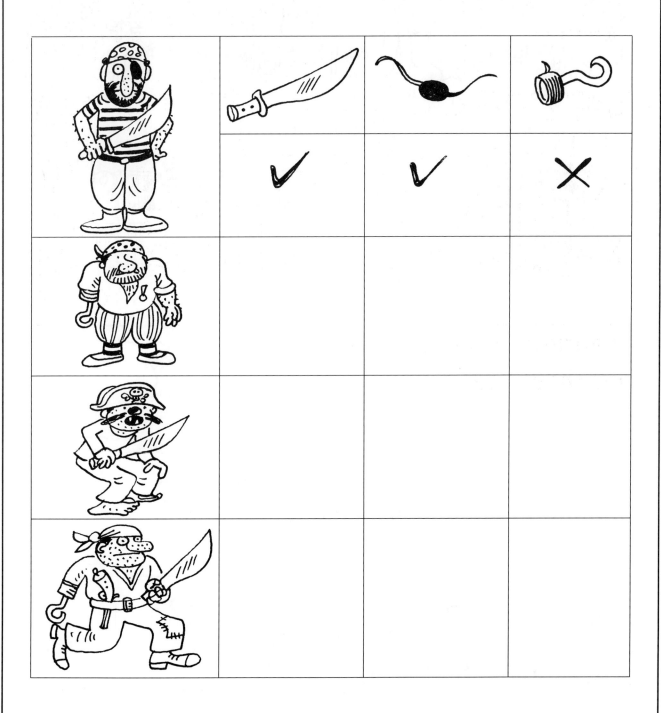

# Name _____

ELFIN CAVES
OPEN DAILY
10.00 a.m. — 5.00 p.m.

Entrance

SOUVENIRS
POST CARDS

cards    12p
stamps    19p

☆ICES☆
COLD
DRINKS
CREAM TEAS
SANDWICHES

SQUASH    18p
TEA       15p
COFFEE    20p

TICKETS

Adults    50p
Children   25p

How much for a cup of tea? ☐

When do the caves open? ☐

How much for a post card? ☐

How much for a child? ☐

_____

Book C

data: chart

| Name | | Jo's baby | | |
| --- | --- | --- | --- | --- |
| Name | boy | girl | weight | name |
| Wilf | | ✓ | 3.3 kg | Oprah |
| Wilma | ✓ | | 3.2 kg | Justin |
| Chip | | ✓ | 4.7 kg | Vicky |
| Biff | | ✓ | 3.4 kg | Alice |
| Kipper | ✓ | | 7.6 kg | Duke |
| Mum | ✓ | | 3.1 kg | Junior |
| Dad | ✓ | | 3.9 kg | Alfie |
| Mr. Robinson | | | | |
| Mrs. Robinson | | | | |
| Mrs. May | | | | |

How many wanted a boy? ☐

How many wanted a girl? ☐

Did Chip want a girl or boy? ..............

Who wanted the name Justin? ..............

What name did Biff want? ..............

Who wanted the name Duke? ..............

# Name _____

## Write 3 sums to match each number.

10–5
3+2
6–1

assessment: addition and subtraction

# Name

## Draw a pattern for each shield.

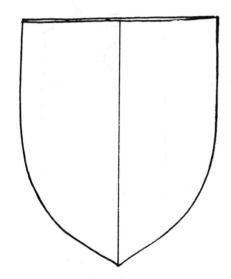 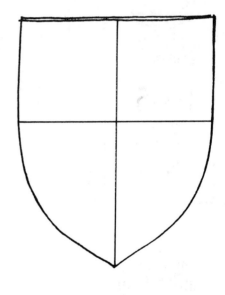

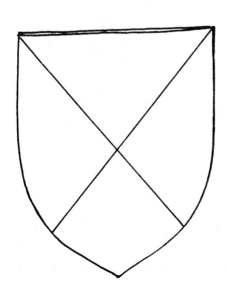 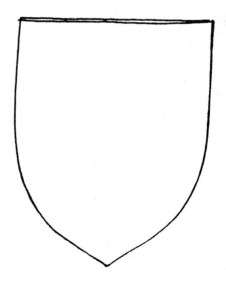

assessment: drawing patterns

Name

# What shapes can you spy?

I spy ☐ cubes.

I spy ☐ spheres.

Tick the shapes with flat faces.

Ring the shapes with curved faces.

assessment: 3D shapes recognition and properties